OUT OF THIS WORLD

CONTENTS

STELLAR PIECES

To create spectacular space models, think about what sort of bricks you'll need. Curved pieces, moving parts, metallic details, and antennas will give your models a sleek, space-age look. Here are some LEGO® pieces that may come in handy if you have them, but look through your own bricks and you're sure to find many more!

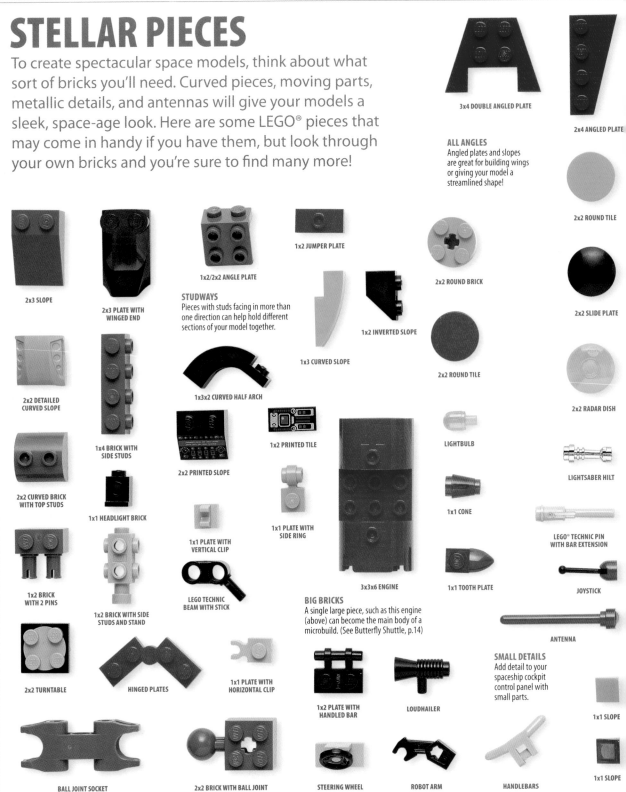

3x4 DOUBLE ANGLED PLATE

2x4 ANGLED PLATE

ALL ANGLES
Angled plates and slopes are great for building wings or giving your model a streamlined shape!

2x2 ROUND TILE

2x2 SLIDE PLATE

2x2 RADAR DISH

2x3 SLOPE

2x3 PLATE WITH WINGED END

1x2/2x2 ANGLE PLATE

1x2 JUMPER PLATE

2x2 ROUND BRICK

STUDWAYS
Pieces with studs facing in more than one direction can help hold different sections of your model together.

1x2 INVERTED SLOPE

1x3 CURVED SLOPE

2x2 ROUND TILE

2x2 DETAILED CURVED SLOPE

1x3x2 CURVED HALF ARCH

1x4 BRICK WITH SIDE STUDS

2x2 PRINTED SLOPE

1x2 PRINTED TILE

LIGHTBULB

LIGHTSABER HILT

2x2 CURVED BRICK WITH TOP STUDS

1x1 HEADLIGHT BRICK

1x1 PLATE WITH VERTICAL CLIP

1x1 PLATE WITH SIDE RING

1x1 CONE

LEGO® TECHNIC PIN WITH BAR EXTENSION

1x2 BRICK WITH 2 PINS

1x2 BRICK WITH SIDE STUDS AND STAND

LEGO TECHNIC BEAM WITH STICK

3x3x6 ENGINE

BIG BRICKS
A single large piece, such as this engine (above) can become the main body of a microbuild. (See Butterfly Shuttle, p.14)

1x1 TOOTH PLATE

JOYSTICK

ANTENNA

2x2 TURNTABLE

HINGED PLATES

1x1 PLATE WITH HORIZONTAL CLIP

1x2 PLATE WITH HANDLED BAR

LOUDHAILER

SMALL DETAILS
Add detail to your spaceship cockpit control panel with small parts.

1x1 SLOPE

BALL JOINT SOCKET

2x2 BRICK WITH BALL JOINT

STEERING WHEEL

ROBOT ARM

HANDLEBARS

1x1 SLOPE

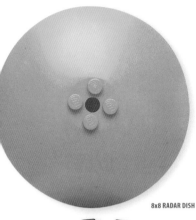

8x8 RADAR DISH

1x4 TILE

NEW IDEAS
If a piece makes you think of an idea for a specific vehicle, get building! This orange radar dish makes a great flying saucer. (See Flying Saucer, p.15)

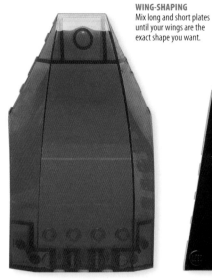

WING-SHAPING
Mix long and short plates until your wings are the exact shape you want.

2x4 PLATE WITH SIDE VENTS

1x2x3 WALL ELEMENT

6x10x2 WINDSHIELD

3x12 ANGLED PLATE

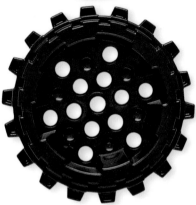

SPIKED WHEEL

CHOOSE AN UNUSUAL WINDSHIELD FOR YOUR COCKPIT AS A STARTING POINT

INSPIRING PARTS
Large or unusually shaped pieces, like a spiked wheel (above) or curved arch brick (below), can help you come up with a design for your model. (See Rocket, pp.24–25)

6x4x2 COCKPIT

GOING GREEN
Once you've chosen a windshield, you could build the rest of the model to match. (See Nova Nemesis, p.13)

FLAG

1x2 GRILLE SLOPE

1x2 GRILLE

1x2 GRILLE

1x2 GRILLE

1x2 PLATE

1x4 HANDLE

AERIAL

1x2x2 LADDER

2x2 RUDDER

INNOVATION
Some pieces are obviously perfect for spaceships, such as turbines, antennas, or aerials, but many other pieces can be adapted and work just as well!

8x8x2 CURVED ARCH BRICK

1x2 PLATE WITH JET ENGINE

2x2 PLATE WITH TURBINE

3

HOVER SCOOTER

When exploring alien worlds, your minifigure might need a small vehicle. But before you get building, ask yourself some simple questions. How will your vehicle travel? Does it roll on wheels, blast around with boosters, or zoom along on jet-powered sleds? What do you want your vehicle to do? It could explore space, build a space base...or even deliver pizza to a hungry rocket crew. Anything is possible!

BUILDING BRIEF
Objective: Create space vehicles
Use: Exploration, transportation
Features: Must be able to hover
Extras: Radar, other comm devices

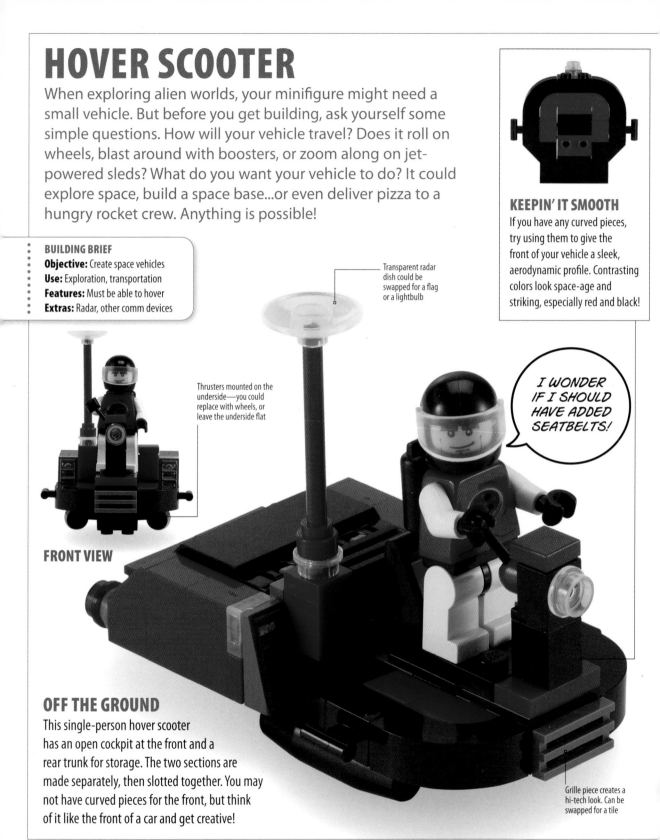

KEEPIN' IT SMOOTH
If you have any curved pieces, try using them to give the front of your vehicle a sleek, aerodynamic profile. Contrasting colors look space-age and striking, especially red and black!

Transparent radar dish could be swapped for a flag or a lightbulb

Thrusters mounted on the underside—you could replace with wheels, or leave the underside flat

FRONT VIEW

I WONDER IF I SHOULD HAVE ADDED SEATBELTS!

OFF THE GROUND
This single-person hover scooter has an open cockpit at the front and a rear trunk for storage. The two sections are made separately, then slotted together. You may not have curved pieces for the front, but think of it like the front of a car and get creative!

Grille piece creates a hi-tech look. Can be swapped for a tile

Joystick allows minifigure pilot to steer the vehicle

SAFE STORAGE
Hinges are very useful pieces. On vehicles, you can use them to allow doors to open, wings to tilt upward or downward, or, as here, a trunk to open. Now just add your intergalactic cargo!

Don't have LEGO pizzas? Fill the trunk with tools, spare parts, or moon rocks

GUARANTEED DELIVERY IN 30 LIGHT-YEARS OR LESS!

Small rocket booster—or you could use this piece as a clip for wings

Red lights made from round transparent plates. Or you could use 1x1 cones or plates

NO STUDS IN SPACE
Using bricks with side studs or angle plates, you can build a section like this red side panel. Attach it sideways so none of the brick studs stick out.

You don't have to use a space-themed minifigure. Alien planets could have breathable atmospheres like Earth

REAR VIEW

SPACE WALKERS

Once you've arrived on a distant planet, your minifigures will want to explore! A walker is the perfect vehicle to scale alien terrain. Remember to build a stable, balanced walker: make sure the cockpit is not too big and heavy for the legs to support it.

BUILDING BRIEF

Objective: Create multi-legged space walkers
Use: Navigating across bumpy planet surfaces
Features: Jointed legs, swiveling cockpit
Extras: Radar, blasters for self-defense

ZZT QXT LKD FFG KKOJH FJFJ! *

* TRANSLATION: IN THIS WALKER, SPACE CRATERS ARE SMALL FRY!

Just flick the robot missiles from the back with your finger to make them fire!

Robot missile launchers made from LEGO Technic beams with sticks

SIDE VIEW

REACHING THE TOP

You can connect the cockpit to the top of the legs using hinges and a flat 2x6 piece. If you have a turntable piece, you can make the cockpit swivel so the pilot can see all around.

SIMPLE WALKER

This simple walker model uses basic hinges to make the legs bend. If you haven't got any hinges, you could build even simpler, straight legs. How about adding a third leg, or even more?

Using two 1x1 round plates to create an "ankle" is a simple way to add detail to your model

Rocket thrusters attached with angle plate

Blasters could be replaced with wings; then the vehicle could walk...or fly!

Toes made from plates with bars. Think about how to use pieces in different ways!

REAR VIEW

Antennas are useful. Be creative—these ones are made from harpoon guns!

ADVANCED WALKER

With more practice and pieces, you can build a walker with extra flexibility and details. Remember, the cockpit can be as simple or as complicated as you like, just so long as your minifigure can sit in it. Adding details, such as antennas, weapons, steering, and control panels, is the really fun bit!

Blaster tips built from green transparent cones. Or you could use 1x1 round transparent pieces, radar dishes, or even loudhailer pieces!

Ball-and-socket joints help shape your walker's legs

Bars, antennas, and even screwdrivers can become rockets and blasters

Control panel made with a printed tile. A plain tile would work well, too

TOP VIEW

Some leg positions work better than others. See what's best for your model

REAR VIEW

Headlight brick

BEST FOOT FORWARD

Look how easily you can make a cool foot with toes (for extra stability on rocky planet surfaces). 1x1 slopes form the toes, and they clip onto headlight bricks.

SPACEFIGHTER

When building a spacefighter, you could start with a single-minifigure cockpit, big pointed wings, multiple rear engines, and big blasters pointing forward for high-speed space duels. Look to your favorite movies or TV shows for inspiration—but don't stop there! Use your imagination to make your model unique and inventive.

BUILDING BRIEF
Objective: Build spacefighters
Use: Intergalactic battles, chases
Features: Lightweight with plenty of speed and firepower
Extras: Force field generators, life-pods, hyperspeed engines

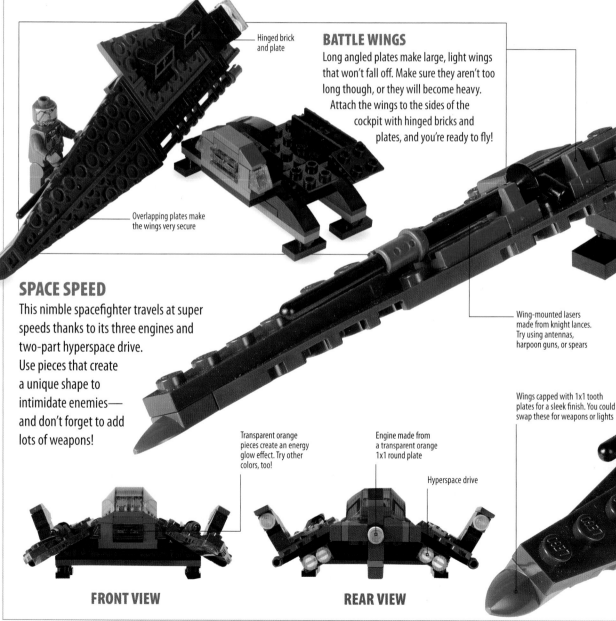

Hinged brick and plate

BATTLE WINGS

Long angled plates make large, light wings that won't fall off. Make sure they aren't too long though, or they will become heavy. Attach the wings to the sides of the cockpit with hinged bricks and plates, and you're ready to fly!

Overlapping plates make the wings very secure

SPACE SPEED

This nimble spacefighter travels at super speeds thanks to its three engines and two-part hyperspace drive. Use pieces that create a unique shape to intimidate enemies— and don't forget to add lots of weapons!

Wing-mounted lasers made from knight lances. Try using antennas, harpoon guns, or spears

Wings capped with 1x1 tooth plates for a sleek finish. You could swap these for weapons or lights

Transparent orange pieces create an energy glow effect. Try other colors, too!

Engine made from a transparent orange 1x1 round plate

Hyperspace drive

FRONT VIEW

REAR VIEW

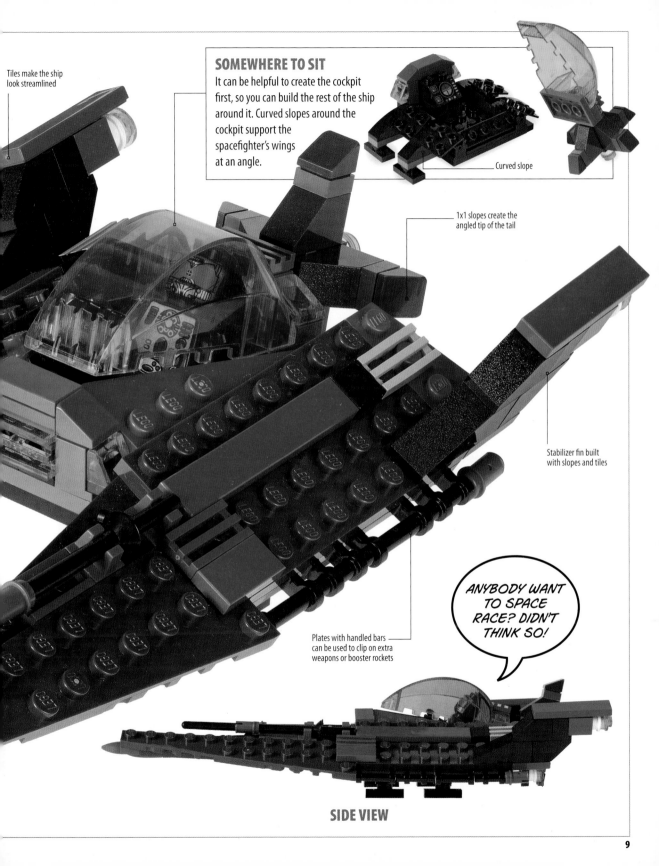

Tiles make the ship look streamlined

SOMEWHERE TO SIT

It can be helpful to create the cockpit first, so you can build the rest of the ship around it. Curved slopes around the cockpit support the spacefighter's wings at an angle.

Curved slope

1x1 slopes create the angled tip of the tail

Stabilizer fin built with slopes and tiles

Plates with handled bars can be used to clip on extra weapons or booster rockets

ANYBODY WANT TO SPACE RACE? DIDN'T THINK SO!

SIDE VIEW

SMALL SPACESHIPS

All you need is a cockpit, some wings, and an engine or two, and you can build a small spaceship that's the perfect size for some serious outer-space adventure. Try to find pieces with unusual shapes to complete your build—and remember, there are no rules about what a spaceship should look like! Here are some ideas to get you started.

ADMIRAL'S INTERCEPTOR

The admiral flies his sleek interceptor into a space battle. The base of the ship is built with the studs facing upward, but the wings are built sideways, with the studs concealed. Landing skids, weapons, and a control pad add detail to the ship.

Choose a piece with an unusual shape to make a fancy tailfin

Curved slopes at the front lend a sleek and speedy look

Angled plates make the spaceship's outline look streamlined

You could add extra pieces to the tip to make a more powerful laser

Racing stripes made by placing plates between bricks of a contrasting color

ALTERNATIVE INTERCEPTOR

This simpler version of the interceptor has wings built with the studs facing up.

Wings are more stable than sideways-built wings

Landing gear—use jumper plates, wheels, or special pieces like minifigure skis

WINGING IT

To create smooth-looking wings, build two small stacks and turn them on their sides. Attach them to the core of the ship with angle plates. Use sloped or curved bricks to give your wings an exciting shape!

1x2/1x4 angle plate

ROCKET SHUTTLE MK I

This nippy little shuttle uses interesting looking pieces for texture, such as grille pieces, plates with bars, and a detailed slope as an engine. Using a plate with the studs facing up also adds to the functional look.

HEY BUDDY, RED AND BLUE IS SO 4036!

A steering wheel or handlebars can help your astronaut get around

Angled plates help the rocket zoom through space

TOP VIEW

Detailed curved slope makes a great engine, but curved slopes would work as well

A wall of bricks could act as a back support instead of this tile with handle

Plates with side bars can be lasers or jets

This grille piece could be a cooling fin. Look out for interesting pieces like this

Transparent plates sandwiched between bricks create a strip of lights

Build up the width of the rocket to make it look very different from your original version

Pieces with side studs allow you to add other pieces to your model

LEGO Technic half pin makes the laser longer

Want to go for firepower instead of speed? Swap out big rocket boosters for extra lasers!

TOP VIEW

ROCKET SHUTTLE MK II

Try upgrading your creations by adding extra pieces. The MK II shuttle has the same basic design as the MK I, but it looks more advanced because of its additional bricks and built-up details.

MORE SMALL SPACESHIPS

There are so many ways to build small space vehicles. You could try grabbing a random handful of pieces and seeing what you can make. You might be amazed! Or look around you at the shapes of everyday objects. They could inspire your creations. Now, get building!

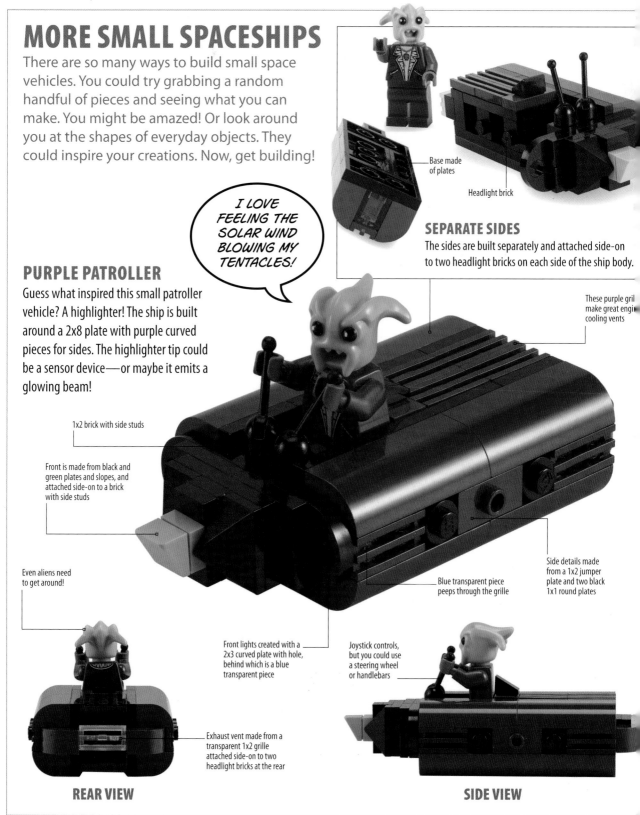

Base made of plates

Headlight brick

SEPARATE SIDES

The sides are built separately and attached side-on to two headlight bricks on each side of the ship body.

> *I LOVE FEELING THE SOLAR WIND BLOWING MY TENTACLES!*

PURPLE PATROLLER

Guess what inspired this small patroller vehicle? A highlighter! The ship is built around a 2x8 plate with purple curved pieces for sides. The highlighter tip could be a sensor device—or maybe it emits a glowing beam!

These purple gril make great engi cooling vents

1x2 brick with side studs

Front is made from black and green plates and slopes, and attached side-on to a brick with side studs

Even aliens need to get around!

Blue transparent piece peeps through the grille

Side details made from a 1x2 jumper plate and two black 1x1 round plates

Front lights created with a 2x3 curved plate with hole, behind which is a blue transparent piece

Joystick controls, but you could use a steering wheel or handlebars

Exhaust vent made from a transparent 1x2 grille attached side-on to two headlight bricks at the rear

REAR VIEW

SIDE VIEW

SIDE VIEW

SIDEWAYS ADVICE

If you're building a section that attaches sideways, don't make it too big or heavy. Without interlocking for extra stability, the link can't hold as much weight.

Make sure the accessories you add are not too heavy either

This 1x4 brick with side studs allows the wing section to be attached

Wing section

OVA NEMESIS

is sinister stealth ship is built around a really cool ckpit windshield piece, with the cockpit and body of e ship designed to match. Use curved or sloping pieces to ve your spaceship an interesting shape—and remember leave enough room in the cockpit for a minifigure and e pilot controls!

These wings are specialized pieces. Just hunt through your bricks for some cool pieces for wings

ndshields come in ny shapes, sizes, d colors. Whichever e you choose will luence the ship u create!

For a sinister look, build your spaceship in dark tones like gray and black

Blaster focusing dish made from two radar dishes

Photon lasers made using transparent cones. They almost look like they are glowing!

Twin turbines propel the ship. These specialized pieces simply clip onto the top of the ship

Pins join the back section to the front

Brick with 2 holes

A QUICK GETAWAY!

A brick with side pins fits into a 1x2 brick with two holes, attaching the two sections together. You could also use these pieces for detachable parts like escape pods!

FRONT VIEW

MICROSHIPS

You may not have a lot of bricks to build with. Or perhaps the space model you want to make would be too complicated at minifigure scale. Or maybe you want a whole fleet of ships for a big space battle. Why not try microbuilding? It is exactly like regular minifigure-scale building but on a smaller scale, and you can assemble some of the coolest—and smallest—spaceships around!

BUILDING WITH HOLES

You'll find that some pieces have holes in them, such as this 1x2 brick with cross axle hole. They are just the right size to grip blasters, antennas, and other accessories.

BUILDING BRIEF

Objective: Build microscale spaceships
Use: Everything a big spaceship does...only smaller!
Features: Must have recognizable spaceship features
Extras: Escort fighters, motherships, space bases

Radio antennas built from accessories like harpoon guns or telescopes

Use antennas, lances, or blasters as weapons

Hinged plates

Microcockpit—use transparent pieces, solid sloped pieces, or even two contrasting 1x1 pieces

Laser weapons— neon transparent pieces look hi-tech

BUTTERFLY SHUTTLE

The wings and body of this microship were built separately, then attached together. The wings are connected to each other with hinged plates, allowing you to fold them at any angle you choose before clipping them onto the main body.

In microscale, a single engine piece can become an entire spaceship body

Lights match the cockpit windshield here—but they can be any color!

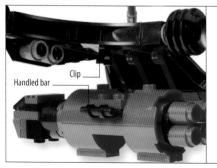

Handled bar

Clip

CLIP-ON WINGS

The wings are built with clips on the underside. These snap onto bars sticking out of the side of the ship's body. It can be tricky to attach the wings, but once they are in place they will look like they are floating!

SIDE VIEW

SPACE HAULER

This Space Hauler transports heavy freight across the galaxy. Round barrels full of cargo clip onto the main body of the hauler. The barrels have been unloaded and replaced so many times, it's no wonder they don't match!

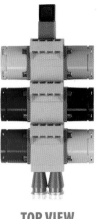

TOP VIEW

Angle plates

The vents at the top and bottom are part of a plate with side vents

Container made by clipping a 2x2 round tile to a 2x2 round brick. 2x2 bricks with tiles would work well, too

CARGO COLUMN

The core of the Space Hauler is a simple column of bricks and plates turned on its side. Angle plates form attachment points for the cargo containers.

Brick with side studs

A group of identical flying saucers with different-colored parts could be a microscale invasion fleet!

FLYING SAUCER

Sometimes you have a piece that you just know would look great as part of a microship. The design of this classic UFO is inspired by a pair of big, orange radar dishes.

INNER WORKINGS

A simple exterior can conceal clever building techniques inside. Here, bricks with side studs support the white curved slopes, and LEGO Technic half pins hold the top and bottom dishes together.

Central ring made of curved slopes attached together to form a circle

Flight wing made from two flag pieces. Rudder pieces would give a similar effect

Radar dish pieces can be engines, cockpits, transmitters, or even landing gear!

Jets or thrusters can be made from chrome pieces, like these LEGO® Star Wars® lightsaber hilts

SHUTTLE AND ESCORTS

For an extra challenge, build a microscale spaceship and then make some even tinier escort vehicles with matching designs to protect it on its interstellar missions!

TOP VIEW

MORE MICROSHIPS

The design of your microship should say as much as possible about its purpose and function. Is your mission one of peaceful exploration? Galactic adventure? Combat and conquest? Think carefully about which pieces will best tell the story—because it only takes a few bricks to build a whole ship!

Aerodynamic tailfins made with grille slopes. Regular slopes would work just as well!

Drone escorts protect the stellar explorer!

This piece can be found in LEGO® Games sets. You could also use a 1x1 cone

STELLAR EXPLORER

This microship may be small, but its design is actually quite complex. Its bricks face in four different directions: up, down, left, and right! Use a central column of bricks with side studs as your starting point. It may take some time to achieve a smooth, sleek look!

Exhaust nozzles made from two radar dishes in contrasting colors

Thrusters made from LEGO Technic T-bars plugged into a 1x1 brick with 4 side studs

THIS COCKPIT'S A PERFECT FIT! BLAST OFF!

Windshield attached to the tail by a clip and bar hinge, so it can open and close

Rudder piece is a good size for a microship wing. You could also use flag pieces, or build wings of different shapes!

TOP VIEW

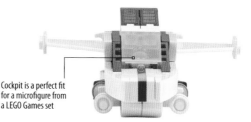

Think these engines are too small? Replace them with one giant engine!

REAR VIEW

Cockpit is a perfect fit for a microfigure from a LEGO Games set

FRONT VIEW

SIDE VIEW

BOTTOM VIEW

This simple build starts with a single 2x4 plate, but you could use a base of any size

STAR CARRIER

The Star Carrier is quite a basic build, but it transports troops and battle vehicles across the galaxy! Plates with horizontal clips hold weapons in place and tiles give a smooth finish.

APPROACHING TARGET FOR OPERATION MICRO!

Harpoon gun is a novel way to attach a radar dish

LEADING THE WAY

A slide plate forms a battering ram at the front—and hides the hollow bottom of the stack. Alternatively, you could use an inverted slope piece to give your cruiser a wedge-nosed shape.

1x1 round plate can be used to dock the microship onto a space station

Engine housings made from LEGO Technic beams with sticks. Swap the transparent pieces for flick-fire space torpedoes!

BATTLE CRUISER

This sturdy, menacing ship is on a mission to smash other microships to smithereens! The battle cruiser is built as a stack of bricks and then turned on its side.

Angled slope

Engine grille

SPACE AMBASSADOR

Friendly colors and curves, and the absence of weaponry, make this spaceship look like it belongs to a peaceful species. This microship is quite simple to build, but there are lots of areas where detail has been added.

BUILDING SECRETS

Bricks with side studs hold the angled slopes and engine grilles in place. Transparent red pieces under the grille slopes make it look like energy is glowing through the vents.

Microcockpit made with 1x1 slope. You could also use a 1x1 plate or a grille piece for an armored cockpit!

Tailfins—this clip could also hold extra weapons, equipment, or even a detachable mini-microship

SMALL TRANSPORTERS

Whether you're carrying supplies or crew, transporters will get your cargo wherever it needs to go. Before you build, think about what you want to transport, how big it is, and what might be needed to hold it in place on the journey. There's a whole galaxy of space stuff out there, and someone's got to haul it all!

FLAT TIRES ARE NO PROBLEM WITH THESE ROCKETS ON BOARD!

Specialized parts like goblets make great headlights

Horizontal clips can hold spare tools and equipment

CARGO HAULER

The cargo hauler is built in two sections: the driver compartment and cargo trailer. For each section, start with a rectangle of bricks as a base and add wheel guards and other details. A ball-and-socket joint attaches the two sections together.

WHEELY FUN

Choose your wheels before building your wheel arches. There's nothing worse than wheels that don't fit!

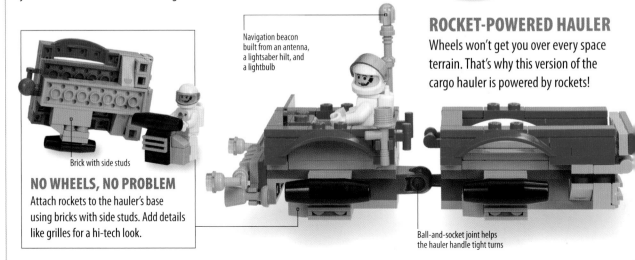

Navigation beacon built from an antenna, a lightsaber hilt, and a lightbulb

ROCKET-POWERED HAULER

Wheels won't get you over every space terrain. That's why this version of the cargo hauler is powered by rockets!

Brick with side studs

NO WHEELS, NO PROBLEM

Attach rockets to the hauler's base using bricks with side studs. Add details like grilles for a hi-tech look.

Ball-and-socket joint helps the hauler handle tight turns

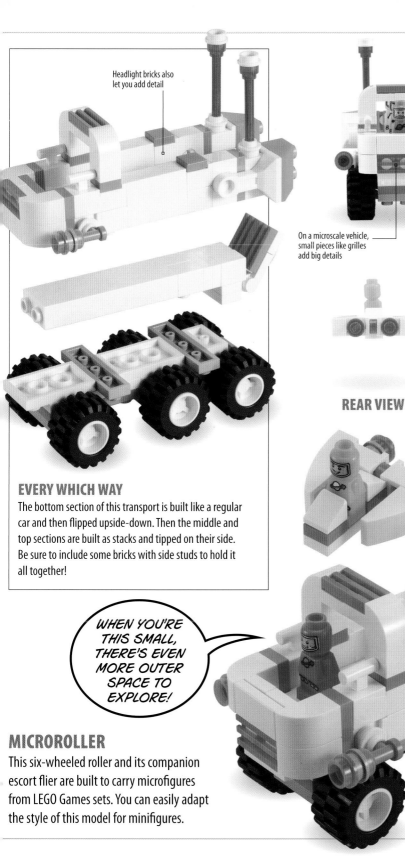

Headlight bricks also let you add detail

Archway separates driver and passenger sections

Tiny companion scooter is made from just a few bricks. A single 1x1 slope creates its angled nose!

FRONT VIEW

On a microscale vehicle, small pieces like grilles add big details

Regular car wheels look impressively huge at microscale

REAR VIEW

This piece can be found in LEGO Games sets

EVERY WHICH WAY

The bottom section of this transport is built like a regular car and then flipped upside-down. Then the middle and top sections are built as stacks and tipped on their side. Be sure to include some bricks with side studs to hold it all together!

WHEN YOU'RE THIS SMALL, THERE'S EVEN MORE OUTER SPACE TO EXPLORE!

MICROROLLER

This six-wheeled roller and its companion escort flier are built to carry microfigures from LEGO Games sets. You can easily adapt the style of this model for minifigures.

The base of the roller's rear thruster is made from a LEGO Star Wars R2-D2 leg!

MOON MINER

When you've got to build a new lunar colony or find valuable space rocks, big mining vehicles are just the thing. Once you've made your rugged mining machine, there are lots of small details to be added. Equip your miner with shovels, claws, saw blades, drills that spin or blast plasma, and anything else it takes to get the job done!

BUILDING BRIEF
Objective: Build space mining vehicles
Use: Moving earth and rocks on other worlds
Features: Power, tools to dig through any surface
Extras: Scout vehicle, robot helpers, storage containers

Emergency beacon built from a telescope and transparent plates

HEY! I CAN SEE THE LUNAR OUTPOST FROM UP HERE!

The mining vehicle's base can hold ore containers or a small scout vehicle

TOP VIEW

Elevated control tower lets the driver keep an eye on the drill's work

Don't forget ladders and handles to help the crew climb to the top!

Laser drill

Oversized wheels are great for bumpy alien terrain. Use the biggest ones you can find for a really heavy-duty digger!

MACHINE WITH A VIEW

The Moon Miner is built in two parts: the base and the control tower. Make sure the base is big enough to fit the laser drill, and that the control tower is the right width so it can clip onto the back corners of the base.

Base platform—build it up higher to hold even more ore containers

A 2x2 brick with pin at each corner holds the wheels. They can also attach tank treads or even walker legs

Hinged lids provide easy access for loading and unloading freshly drilled space crystals

ORE CONTAINERS

Hinged lid pieces are great for building ore containers. You could also use a clip and bar hinge to attach a lid to a base, or even build a lid and base from scratch!

Build the base of your container to match the size and shape of the lid

WAIT, THAT'S NOT AN OUTPOST... THAT'S NEPTUNE!

Black slope

ROLL OF THE DICE

Proving that you really can find a use for any and every piece, the head of the laser drill is actually built around a LEGO Games die piece! You could also use two 2x2 bricks or a stack of plates.

MOON MINER WITH TREADS

Treads can be found on some LEGO construction vehicles. Each link is a separate piece, so you can build them as long or short as you want

Mining robots can be attached to the back of the control tower columns for transport

Green light for when crystals are detected underground. Swap it for a red one if your miners find something they don't want to dig up!

Miniature drills built using palm tree top pieces to match the Moon Miner's drill!

Hi-tech mining device built with a spanner. You could swap a screwdriver or a blaster, for different functions

READY, SET, DRILL!

LEGO Technic beam

An arm built from LEGO Technic parts holds the Moon Miner's laser drill. The arm pivots at two points, allowing the drill to be positioned accurately, or folded neatly away! It is supported by a pair of black 1x1 slopes on the support columns of the control tower.

ROBOTIC VEHICLES

Not all space vehicles need drivers! Just like the Mars missions of today, future interplanetary expeditions could make use of robots for exploration. This geological inspection rover is built around a simple stack of bricks, turned on its side and attached to four wheels. Detailed bricks and lots of tools give the rover a functional appearance!

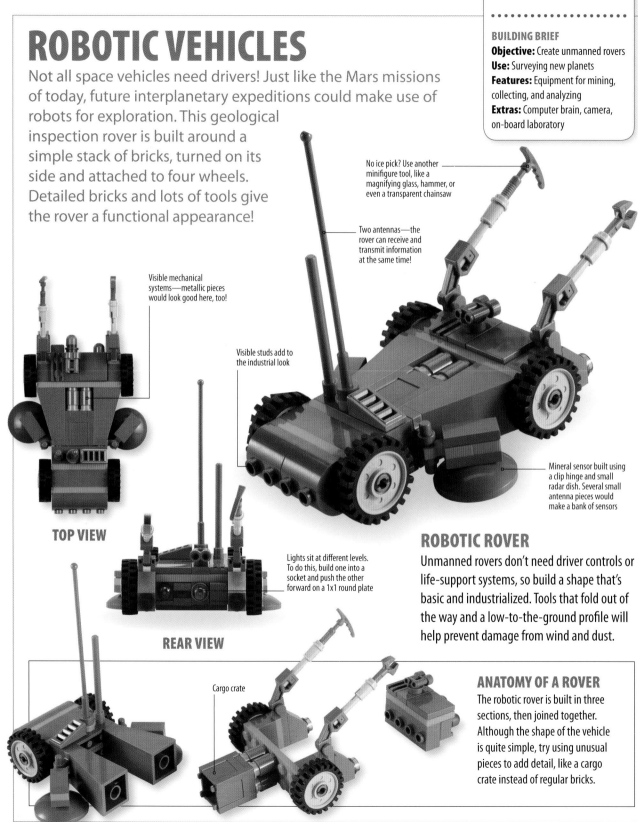

Visible mechanical systems—metallic pieces would look good here, too!

No ice pick? Use another minifigure tool, like a magnifying glass, hammer, or even a transparent chainsaw

Two antennas—the rover can receive and transmit information at the same time!

Visible studs add to the industrial look

TOP VIEW

Mineral sensor built using a clip hinge and small radar dish. Several small antenna pieces would make a bank of sensors

Lights sit at different levels. To do this, build one into a socket and push the other forward on a 1x1 round plate

REAR VIEW

Cargo crate

ROBOTIC ROVER

Unmanned rovers don't need driver controls or life-support systems, so build a shape that's basic and industrialized. Tools that fold out of the way and a low-to-the-ground profile will help prevent damage from wind and dust.

ANATOMY OF A ROVER

The robotic rover is built in three sections, then joined together. Although the shape of the vehicle is quite simple, try using unusual pieces to add detail, like a cargo crate instead of regular bricks.

JETPACKS

What could be more fun than rocketing through space without any need of a spaceship? This is where jetpacks come in, from realistic to wildly inventive. Wings, rockets, jets, blasters—as long as the jetpack can attach to a minifigure, the rest is up to you!

CAVE RACER

This cavern-exploring vehicle has a core of a few bricks with side studs. A row of slopes on top and blade pieces on the wingtips complete its fierce design.

Handlebars connect minifigure to jetpack

Look for thin pieces like these wall elements to make a jetpack's lightweight wings

ROCKET GLIDER

The specialized wing pieces on this jetpack can be found in sets like LEGO® Space Police and LEGO® Batman™. You could also use airplane wings or flag pieces to achieve the same shape.

Minifigure angle plate fits around minifigure's neck and allows jetpack to be clipped on

SPACEWALK PACK

To perform maintenance and repairs on the outside of a space station, you just need a box shape with some tools built into it. Make sure it is the right size for a minifigure!

I JUST NEED TO REMEMBER TO HOLD ON TIGHT!

These gray bars are just the right distance apart for minifigure hands to clip onto

Flames—LEGO sets with knights and castles are a good place to find these pieces! You can also use any fire-colored transparent bricks

SIDE VIEW

REAR VIEW

ROCKET

3...2...1...BLAST OFF! This sleek, streamlined rocket launches straight up and then levels out to fly, so it has a big, flat-bottomed main engine, and a tailfin and wings as well. When building your own rocket models, think about where they will travel and what they will encounter on their outer space adventures!

BUILDING BRIEF

Objective: Build rockets

Use: Vertical blast-off into space

Features: Cone or needle shape with a flat engine underneath

Extras: Wings, detachable boosters, launchpad

Choose a windshield to fit your design

Sensor built into sides to keep rocket's profile smooth and sleek

Grille pieces lock windshield in place in case of bumpy asteroid fields

Curved arch bricks give the central body a circular shape

SPACE FRAME

The central body has a frame built from outward-facing plates and bricks, held together at the corners by four 1x1 bricks with side studs.

1x1 brick with side studs

Bricks with holes

READY FOR LAUNCH

The front section of the rocket is built with curved wedge pieces and the back section has airplane features, giving the model a streamlined, tube-like shape that looks like it could blast right up into space.

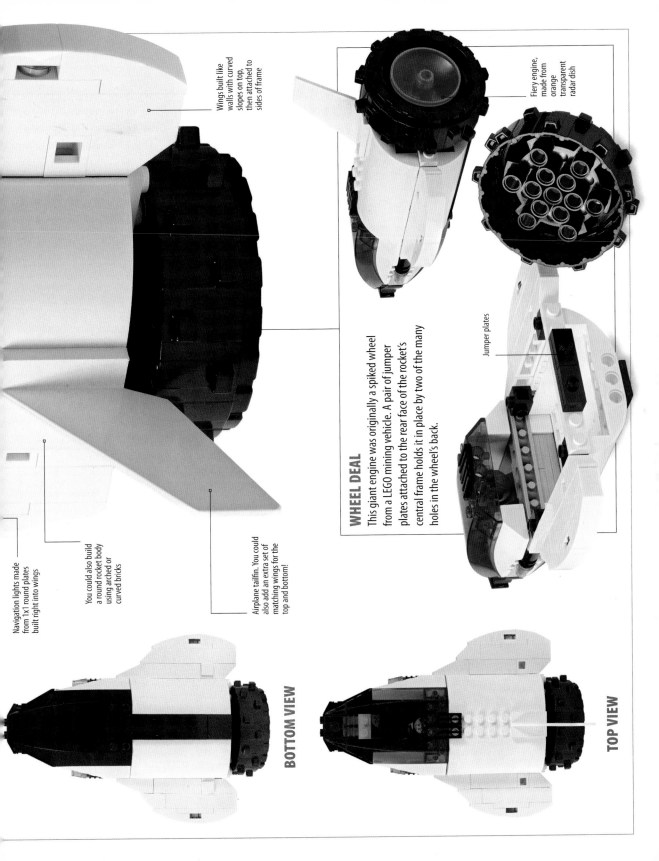

Wings built like walls with curved slopes on top, then attached to sides of frame

Fiery engine, made from orange transparent radar dish

Jumper plates

WHEEL DEAL

This giant engine was originally a spiked wheel from a LEGO mining vehicle. A pair of jumper plates attached to the rear face of the rocket's central frame holds it in place by two of the many holes in the wheel's back.

Navigation lights made from 1x1 round plates built right into wings

You could also build a round rocket body using arched or curved bricks

Airplane tailfin. You could also add an extra set of matching wings for the top and bottom!

BOTTOM VIEW

TOP VIEW

ALIENS

When it comes to building alien creatures, if you can imagine it, you can make it. Think about what kind of planet your alien lives on and how it should behave, and then start building your idea of life on the distant world. Try looking at real animals for inspiration and using the most unusual pieces you can find to make your creations look truly out of this world!

BUILDING BRIEF
Objective: Create alien creatures
Use: Friend or foe to space explorers
Features: Limbs for swimming, flying, hopping, climbing...you name it!
Extras: Claws, fangs, suckers, wings, tails, extra limbs

Creepy glowing eyes are red transparent plates. Glow-in-the-dark pieces would work well, too, and some can be found in LEGO® Harry Potter™ sets

Round, scaly belly made from a 2x2 round plate in a contrasting color

SWAMP HOPPER

Green frog-like skin, a long tail, and webbed toes show that this alien comes from a watery world. A printed tile with a car grille pattern creates an extraterrestrial face with two mouths. Don't forget to position the arms and tail so it can balance while standing up!

FRONT VIEW

Don't have this flexible tail piece? Try a long, flat plate and add spikes and other details!

Webbed feet are flipper pieces. You could also use a 1x2 plate

EXTRA DIRECTIONS

1x1 plates with side rings are used to attach the arms and legs to the alien's body. These useful pieces enable you to build in three different directions: up, forward, and backward.

Plates with side rings

Smooth pieces can be swapped for spiky or textured bricks

Adding a different color accentuates key details like the alien's knees

REAR VIEW

ASTEROID INSECTIPEDE

A segmented body and lots of legs make a creature look armored and insect-like. Each of this alien's six limbs are attached to a jumper plate on its body by a single stud, so they can rotate and be posed to look like it's walking or running.

1x1 round plate can be swapped with a 1x1 slope for a zigzag back or an antenna piece for tall spines

Tail made from antenna. Try using flexible tubes, or tail pieces instead!

Each leg is made from just three pieces, so it's easy to duplicate for each body segment

Jumper plate

Painted eyes are maracas from the LEGO® Minifigures series

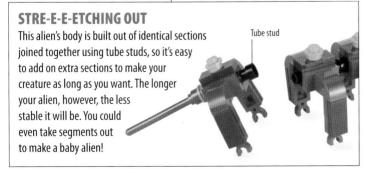

TOP VIEW

Eye stalks made from a robot arm piece that is perfect for angled moving parts

REAR VIEW

STRE-E-E-ETCHING OUT

This alien's body is built out of identical sections joined together using tube studs, so it's easy to add on extra sections to make your creature as long as you want. The longer your alien, however, the less stable it will be. You could even take segments out to make a baby alien!

Tube stud

Two pairs of binoculars and four horns make a dangerous-looking set of jaws

FRONT VIEW

DK | Penguin Random House

Editor Shari Last
Additional Editors Jo Casey, Hannah Dolan, Emma Grange,
Matt Jones, Catherine Saunders, Lisa Stock, Victoria Taylor
Senior Editor Laura Gilbert
Designer Owen Bennett
Additional Designers Lynne Moulding, Robert Perry,
Lisa Sodeau, Ron Stobbart, Rhys Thomas, Toby Truphet
Jacket Designer David McDonald
Senior Designer Nathan Martin
Senior DTP Designer Kavita Varma
Producer Lloyd Robertson
Managing Editor Simon Hugo
Design Manager Guy Harvey
Creative Manager Sarah Harland
Art Director Lisa Lanzarini
Publisher Julie Ferris
Publishing Director Simon Beecroft

Photography by Gary Ombler,
Brian Poulsen, and Tim Trøjborg

Acknowledgments
Dorling Kindersley would like to thank: Stephanie Lawrence, Randi Sørensen, and
Corinna van Delden at the LEGO Group; Sebastiaan Arts, Tim Goddard, Deborah
Higdon, Barney Main, Duncan Titmarsh (www.bright-bricks.com), and Andrew
Walker for their amazing models; Jeff van Winden for additional building; Daniel
Lipkowitz for his fantastic text; Gary Ombler, Brian Poulsen, and Tim Trøjborg for
their brilliant photography; Rachel Peng and Bo Wei at IM Studios;
and Sarah Harland for editorial assistance.

First published in the United States in 2015 by DK Publishing
345 Hudson Street, New York, New York 10014

Contains material previously published in
The LEGO® Ideas Book (2011)

003—284611—Mar/15

Page design copyright © 2015 Dorling Kindersley Limited.
A Penguin Random House Company.

A WORLD OF IDEAS:
SEE ALL THERE IS TO KNOW